AZ

of assemblies

# of assemblies

26 ready-to-use assemblies for 9-13 year olds

Caroline Vallance

First published in 2001 by
KEVIN MAYHEW LTD
Buxhall
Stowmarket
Suffolk IP14 3BW
Email: info@kevinmayhewltd.com

9 8 7 6 5 4 3 2 1 0

ISBN 1 84003 772 5
Catalogue No 1500444

Cover design by Jonathan Stroulger
Edited and typeset by Elisabeth Bates
Printed and bound in Great Britain

Contents

Introduction

Going into a school can be a daunting and sometimes scary privilege. Today's legislation and multiracial society can make assembly-taking a difficult path to walk, but so many schools are willing to allow Christians in to take assemblies that we should surely take the opportunity offered to us. As long as we are sensitive, and true to the school's expectations as well as our own, assemblies can be great fun and an excellent way of sharing Jesus with lots of children. Many assemblies are only 10 minutes long which is why these are short, snappy and to the point – there is no time for any more.

All the assemblies in this book have been tried out in front of children mostly between the ages of 9 and 13. They are open to adaptation and development to suit the audience you are talking to – what works well for one group may not work so well with another.

Please use the ideas. If this book helps one person introduce children and young people to Jesus in a fun relevant way then it has been worth doing.

Enjoy using it and sharing Jesus with the children in our schools.

Praying

Prayers have been included for each assembly but feel free to use your own. Some schools prefer you to start with, 'I am going to pray now – if you want to make this your prayer too, then join in with the Amen at the end.' Be sensitive.

Songs

Songs have been suggested for each assembly, all of them have been taken from the *Kidsource* songbook, compiled by Capt. Alan Price and published by Kevin Mayhew. Again you may like to choose one of your own or ask the school to come up with something that fits your theme – be flexible. It's sad to see that a lot of children in school don't enjoy singing any more so if you can make this time fun and enjoyable, that's great! If you don't play and there is no music teacher to help, backing tracks can be a good way to introduce songs into assemblies.

All tied up

Aim

To help think about the fact that Jesus can set us free.

Requirements

Large ball of string (don't use wool – it will break too easily)
Scissors
If you can get hold of a straitjacket this will work even better – substitute a key for the scissors!)

Volunteers

1

Talk to the children about lies that we tell and ones that are told to us. Ask them for some examples. As a child gives you an example, wind the string around your volunteer until you run out of suggestions – or string! Make a big show of tying lots of knots. Ask the volunteer how they feel and give them a chance to wriggle free. (If you wind the string tight enough – without causing injury or strangulation – they shouldn't be able to get free.)

Application

I would think we all tell lies at one time or another. Some people say it's OK to tell a small white lie (one that we think doesn't really count as a bad lie) – it won't hurt – but, after a while, if we are not careful, one lie can lead to another, and another, until we are so tangled up we don't know what is true and what is a lie and we can't get ourselves out. It is the same with the lies we can hear as we grow up – e.g. we are only worth something if we are rich or famous or pretty or wear the right things – these can leave us in a tangle and unsure what to believe.

The Bible says that God knows all about us, he knew us even before we were born, and he knows straight away when we are telling lies. The Bible also says a lot about speaking the truth.

Christians believe that because Jesus died and came alive again, he can help us when we get ourselves in a mess. We can tell him that we are sorry, and he'll forgive us and help us to tell the truth. (Cut the person free.) It's as easy as that!

When you are going around school today and are tempted not to tell the truth, remember it may be easier to lie, but it can lead into all sorts of trouble. Try telling the truth instead!

Prayer

Dear God,
Please help us today to have the courage to tell the truth and not to lie, whatever we are faced with.
Amen.

Suggested songs

161 – I'm sorry
196 – Jesus is greater

Being true to myself

Aim	To help the children understand that it's OK to stand up for what they believe – even if it's different from other people's beliefs.
Requirements	Bin liners Sellotape Scissors
Volunteers	8 in two teams

There seems to be all sorts of pressure on people these days – pressures to do what everyone else is doing, even if we are not sure it is right. One of the biggest pressures is about what we wear. Do we have the right trainers, trousers, and designer labels? I'm going to give you the chance this morning to make sure two pupils in this school are wearing the right clothes – because you are going to make them some to wear.

Give the two teams about 5 minutes to make one member an outfit. Get the whole school to vote on which one is best.

Application

As I said before, there are all sorts of pressures on us these days. Not just what we wear but how we act – rightly or wrongly, the things we watch on TV, the sort of music we listen to, the language we use – I'm sure you can come up with a whole list of things.

It's not difficult to do what everyone else is doing. It takes real strength, though, to stand up for what you think is right. Sometimes we do what everyone else is doing just to survive, to keep our friends, even if we really want to be going in the other direction, against the flow.

You know going against the flow may have its benefits – it's possible the crowd might be going in the wrong direction and heading for trouble.

Christians believe that when we have to stand up for what we know is right, God will give us the strength we need, we just have to ask him. It doesn't mean that it will be easy – it will be hard at first, but you might find that after a while, people start to respect you and your views and begin to change themselves.

Is there something you are doing that you need to stop? Why not start today, have the strength to stand up for what is right – remember, all those other people might be heading in the wrong direction.

Prayer

Dear God,
Please help us to stand up for what is right, even when we find it really hard.
Amen.

Suggested songs

156 – I'm putting God's armour on
352 – We are the Lord's kids

Christmas gargle

Aim
To help the children understand what Christians believe about Christmas.

Requirements
3 glasses of water
Party hats
Something for the floor!

Volunteers
3

Ask the volunteers if they have a favourite carol/song that they enjoy hearing at Christmas. Assure them that they won't have to sing. Make sure they don't tell anyone what the tune is.

In turn give each of them a glass of water and ask them to gargle their song. Ask the rest of the school to guess what they think the song is.

Application
Christmas is a great time for having fun. Singing carols, presents, getting together with our families, eating loads, the list could go on and on.

Christians believe that Christmas is more than that. It's about the best present given to people – ever. God's Son, Jesus.

Christians believe that Jesus came to show us just how much God loves people and how much he wants to be friends with them.

So amongst the fun and games this Christmas, just stop and think what it's all about – the biggest and best present ever – and let's enjoy Christmas even more because of it.

Prayer
Dear God
Thank you for Christmas. Thank you for fun and presents and being

with our family and friends. Please help us not to forget why we celebrate Christmas. Thank you for Jesus, the best present ever. Amen.

Suggested songs   26 – Christmas, it's Christmas
35 – Crackers and turkeys

Discovery

Aim

To find things out for yourself, not to believe everything others tell you.

Requirements

A selection of objects (including a Bible)
Blindfold

Volunteers

2

Send one of the volunteers out of the room and blindfold the other. Tell your first volunteer that you are going to hand them five objects to identify. They can feel the objects and then they can either smell, taste or ask one question about each object.

Repeat the exercise with the second volunteer and announce a winner. The Bible should be the fifth object offered to each volunteer.

Application

It is very difficult to have an opinion about something if we only know a little bit about it. If we want to know more we need to look into it for ourselves. Perhaps there is someone in your class or year whom at first glance you think you could never be friends with, but if you take time out to chat with them and find out a bit more about them you might just find things out that make you change your mind.

You might say about a certain lesson or sport, 'That's just boring' or 'I'll never be any good at that', but you might find that when you really look into it and have a go that it's much better and more fun than you first thought.

The last object the volunteers tried to guess this morning was a Bible. Many people dismiss God as old and boring before they've had time to find things out about him for themselves. People like the triple-jumper Jonathan Edwards, the pop group Eternal (you may want to choose people relevant to your audience) and people all over the world and perhaps even in this school have taken time out to discover God for themselves.

Why not make a promise to yourself this term that you won't dismiss people, things and activities without considering them properly first – and that includes God.

Prayer

Dear God,
Please help us to be the sort of people who find out the full facts about something and then make the right decisions.
Amen.

Suggested songs

252 – Mind the gap
278 – Open our eyes
327 – There is so much to discover

Evil to good?

Aim

To think about the fact Jesus can change people if we let him and that Easter is about forgiveness.

Requirements

4 large pieces of card with L, E, V, and I on them. (Make sure they are big enough for the people at the back to see.)

Volunteers

4 (to hold the cards and spell out the relevant words as you come to them)

When you turn on the TV or Playstation you are often confronted by the latest villain or hero. Who can name some? Are they a villain or hero?

Do you think it is possible for someone to change from one to the other?

It was a fine sunny day. The crowd had flocked in their hundreds to the side of the lake to hear the man everyone was talking about – a man who said amazing things and did amazing things – they couldn't wait. Sitting by himself a little way from the crowd was a man called LEVI. LEVI didn't have any friends, you see he was EVIL. How can I describe him? Not the sort of person you would take home to tea or invite to your birthday party. He was the sort of person who would kick sand in your face at the beach or steal your football. He was VILE.

So the crowd was waiting patiently for Jesus, and so was VILE, EVIL, LEVI.

And soon Jesus came towards the crowd. He saw the sights, smelled the smells, ate the ice-creams – well not quite – but as Jesus came to the crowd his eyes were fixed on VILE, EVIL, LEVI. Jesus ignored everyone else and went straight up to LEVI. You see because LEVI was EVIL and VILE there was a barrier between him and God. Another word for barrier, one you might find in the Bible, is VEIL. So Jesus went to LEVI and told him to say sorry to God for being cruel and nasty, so that God could forgive him and he could start to LIVE his life as God wanted. And that's what LEVI did. He changed from being EVIL and VILE, and the VEIL between him and God was gone and he really started to LIVE – the day he met Jesus.

Application

And that's why Christians all over the world celebrate Easter. They believe that we are all a bit like Levi – we might not be vile and evil but we've all done things wrong at one time or another. They believe that because Jesus died and came alive again, anyone can be forgiven and change – just like Levi. How easy do you find it to forgive someone. Perhaps there's someone you need to forgive today – why not give it a go – you might be surprised at the results.

Prayer

Dear God,
Help us to be the sort of people who are prepared to forgive others.
Amen.

Suggested songs

130 – If we admit to God
327 – There is so much to discover

Free to a good home!

Aim

To show that every human being is special and important.

Requirements

Either objects that represent the chemicals and objects below or pictures to illustrate them.

Volunteers

1 (Find out as much about them as you can.)

Auction the volunteer off to the highest bidder (stop if the bidding starts getting silly).

So, what are we actually worth – would finding out what we are made up of help us to decide? (As you talk about each object, hand it to the volunteer.)

Fat – 7 bars soap

Iron – 1 medium-sized nail

Potash – sufficient to blow up one toy train

Sulphur – enough to rid 1 dog of fleas

Phosphorus – enough to make 4000 matches

Sugar – enough for 7 cups of tea

Magnesium – enough for 1 dose of salts

Lime – enough to paint 1 dog house

So, how much does all this add up to? Ask for ideas. The total sum is £7.13.

Application

We live in a world where the underlying message seems to be that the more money, better looks, greater job and bigger house you have, the more important you are, and vice versa.

The football transfer market appears to show clearly just how much someone is worth, with large amounts of money being paid for one player.

Christians believe that God puts an even greater value on us than that – and it doesn't matter what we look like, are good at or own. Christians believe that God values every human person that has ever been born so much that he was prepared to sacrifice his Son so that humans could have friendship with him.

Next time you look at one of your friends, remember – they are worth more than any money could buy; special and important, unique – a one off! – and that goes for you too!

Prayer

Dear God,
Thank you that everyone here is special to you. Help us to remember that in the way we treat others.
Amen.

Suggested songs

162 – I'm special
165 – I'm your child

Gladiators – ready?

Aim
To show we need to be careful about the sort of people we follow and be prepared to stand up for what is right.

Requirements
Gladiator equipment
Prize: choose something healthy to reflect the theme.

Volunteers
3 or 4 (It is great if you can persuade a teacher to be one of the volunteers.)

Give the volunteers various challenges to do, e.g. star jumps, sit-ups, running on the spot, and see who can complete the tasks the quickest. Give a prize to the winner.

People these days are often out to prove they are bigger and better, stronger and cleverer than anyone else. Different groups form because people fancy themselves as leaders, and people with the same beliefs tend to come together. They might be supporters of a football team, a political party, a religious belief.

Tell the story of Elijah on Mount Carmel (1 Kings 18).

Application
We need to be careful about the sort of people we follow, some can be quite harmless, others may be dangerous or get us into trouble. Sometimes when we are asked to do things we know are wrong – picking on people, stealing, lying – we need to try and be brave and, like Elijah, stand out from the crowd and say 'no'. It takes courage to stand up for what you know is right, but the really great people in history are those who have stood up for what is right, even when the going got tough.

Prayer
Dear God,
Help us to have the courage to stand up for what we know is right, even when it gets tough.
Amen.

Suggested songs   277 – Let's get fit
                      371 – When a knight won his spurs

Haves and have-nots

Aim
To show that money isn't everything and to think about how we treat people with it or without it.

Requirements
Various objects that represent items you might buy, e.g. holiday brochure, CD cover, football scarf, etc.

Volunteers
1

Pretend that the volunteer has just won the Lottery – what would you suggest that they buy? (Load up the volunteer with objects.)

Money is important; most people use it to buy important things like food and clothes and somewhere to live. However, it's easy to fall into the trap of thinking, 'I wish I had more money' or 'I wish I could buy that new . . .', or that some people are more important than others because they have more money. Some people really believe that all their problems could be solved if they had more money.

If this were true, why are some of the richest people in the world so unhappy? Why do some people who win the Lottery say it is the worst thing that has ever happened to them and that their wealth has made them more miserable?

The trouble is that the love of money can become a real burden. (Dismiss volunteer.)

Application
Listen to what the apostle Paul said in the Bible:

We brought nothing into the world, so we can take nothing out. But if we have God and clothes we will be satisified with that. Those who want to be rich bring temptation to themselves and are caught in a trap. They want many foolish and harmful things that ruin and destroy people. The love of money causes all kinds of evil. (1 Timothy 6:7-10)

Paul wasn't saying that having money is wrong; but to love money and be greedy for more can end up spoiling a person's life.

It is also wrong to treat someone differently just because they are rich or poor – it's what's inside that really matters – the person, not what they have.

Do you think being rich could make you happy – or are there more important things in life?

Prayer

Dear God,
Help us to be thankful for the things we have.
Amen.

Suggested songs

222 – Jesus, you're the King
266 – Oh! Oh! Oh! how good is the Lord

It's just not fair!

Aim	To think about what's fair and what's not.
Requirements	Lego or modelling clay Blindfold
Volunteers	3
Competition	Tell the volunteers they have three minutes to build something. Just as you are about to say 'Go' tell them the competition is too fair, so leave one volunteer as normal, ask one to put their hands behind their back, and blindfold the other.
	Go!
	How often do we say 'It's not fair' to something?
	I have to go to bed before my friends
	I have all this homework to do
	I can't stay up late
	I can't watch what I want on TV
	There is no food in my country
	My brother lost a leg on a land mine
	I get laughed at because I wear glasses
	People won't talk to me because I look different
	I'm always the last person to get picked in PE
	Lots of people say, 'It's not fair' just when things aren't going their way. Other people, though, have the right to say it because of the way they've been treated or the country they've been born in, or just because they seem different.
Application	In the Old Testament part of the Bible we can read about a man called Amos who was told by God to speak out against injustice,

and to help those for whom life was unfair. It wasn't easy for him and he made enemies, but he also made a huge difference to the lives of the people he helped.

There are things in the world that we just can't change, but we have a responsibility to try and change things we can. There are all sorts of people around us for whom life isn't fair. Could you make a difference for them today?

How? – ask for ideas. (You may have to have some prepared beforehand.)

Why not put some of those ideas into practice today.

Prayer

Dear God,
Help us not to moan about things being unfair. Help us to make a difference when we can.
Amen.

Suggested songs

248 – Make me a channel of your peace
290 – Safe in the Father's hands

Just don't chew

Aim   To think about self-control.

Requirements   A packet of fruit pastilles.

Volunteers   4

Competition   Ask the four volunteers if they can eat a fruit pastille without chewing it?

Many people think the world is going wrong. If only people stopped and thought about the needs of others, the world would be a better place.

This is what the Bible says we need for that to happen:

But the Spirit produces the fruit of love, joy, peace, patience, goodness, gentleness, faithfulness, kindness and self-control. (Galatians 5:22)

What a list! And what on earth has that to do with chewing fruit pastilles? The link comes with the last of that list – self-control. It takes control not to chew something that just needs chewing – it's hard. And so is keeping control in our everyday lives. But if we manage to use it, it can help us be the other things in that list as well. If we are self-controlled we'll have more patience, we'll be kinder to people and that will help us in our lives too.

Application   How can we be self-controlled? (Ask the children – have some answers prepared.)

Why not try it today – exercise some self-control and see what a difference it makes!

Prayer   Dear God,
Help us to be self-controlled today in all that we say and do.
Amen.

Suggested songs   124 – I can do all, all things
301 – So I've made up my mind

Knowing me, knowing you

Aim Thinking about the words we use.

Requirements A book of babies' names and meanings.

Before the assembly either choose some names of children you know will be in the assembly and find out the meanings of their names, or buy a babies' name book (it is worth choosing a few names before you go into the assembly as some meanings of names aren't very polite!)

Start by choosing some people from the assembly and running a quiz to see if people can work out what each person's name means from what they know about the person.

Application People's names are really important. Parents take a lot of time and care choosing a name for their new baby. Some of you may know where your name came from. In olden days and other societies what was really important to new parents was the meaning of the name they were giving their new baby.

A person's name is really important, it makes them the person they are, it gives them significance and value. This means we need to take care about the way we use people's names.

Nicknames can be fun, but can also be unkind and hurtful, taking away value from a person. Our names are important and should be used properly.

It's not just names that we need to be careful how we use. Our words can be very powerful things and yet so often we speak before we think.

Listen to what it says in the Bible about the words that we use:

It only takes a spark, remember, to set off a forest fire. A careless or wrongly placed word out of your mouth can do that. By our speech we can ruin the world, turn harmony to chaos, throw mud on a reputation, send the whole world up in smoke and go up in smoke with it . . . (James 3:6)

Let's just take a moment to be quiet and think:

Is there anyone whose name I've used wrongly either by an unkind nickname or by spreading gossip? Is there anything I've said to someone that might have started an argument? Do I need to go and put it right?

Prayer

Dear God,
Thank you that our names make us the people we are. Help us today to think before we speak.
Amen.

Suggested songs

42 – Don't repay evil for evil
248 – Make me a channel of your peace

Let's listen . . .

Aim

To think about the way we judge people and things on first impressions.

Requirements

A tape recorder and tape of sound effects.

Sound effects quiz

Have some sound effects prerecorded on a tape and see how many the school can guess. Don't have too many easy ones!

Our five senses are some of the most important aspects of our bodies. Can you name them? (Sight, smell, hearing, touch, taste.) In fact our bodies work in such a way that if we lose one of those senses often one of the others works better to compensate.

Sometimes, though, it is hard to work things out if we are using only one of our senses – as we did in the sound effects quiz. Only listening to the sounds and not being able to see them made it quite hard to work out exactly what was going on because our senses were made to work together.

Application

How often do we go through life making judgements on things about which we only know a little – perhaps because we've only heard what other people have said about something or someone, or we've just used our eyes and watched what was going on and not got the whole picture.

People do it with God and Christianity all the time – make judgements without looking into the full facts for themselves. This week you may hear and experience lots of things about Christianity and Christians, some things you have heard before, perhaps some things that are new. Why not check out the things that you see and hear and investigate for yourselves.

(This is a good assembly to use at the start of a new year to publicise a Christian Union or an event that your church is running.)

Prayer
Dear God,
Help us to find out the full facts about something before we make
a decision about it.
Amen.

Suggested songs
23 – Can you count the stars?
43 – Don't you worry about tomorrow

My gift is better than yours!

Aim

To think about the fact that everyone is important, regardless of what they're good at.

Requirements

3 balls

Modelling balloons

4 pieces of paper with one of the following tasks written on each:

    Juggle 3 balls

    What is 150 + 130 – 60 x 2?

    Do an impression of a Spice Girl (or other relevant pop star)

    Make something from modelling balloons

Volunteers

4

Tell the volunteers they will have the choice of four tasks, one mental, one involving making something and two involving performing – the catch is they won't know which task is which until they come to the front. (Make a big thing about the fact that it is taking part and having a go that is important, not whether you can do the task or not.) Let each person choose a piece of paper with a task on it and read it out to the rest of the school.

Ask the school to vote as to whether they think the person can do the task or not before the person attempts it.

Afterwards, tell the volunteers that they were very brave. It's not easy trying to do something when people have expectations of you.

The exciting thing about people is that we are all different. Some of us would have been able to do those tasks – some of us would not. It would be a very boring world if everyone was the same and good at the same thing.

Application

There are two things I want us to think about this morning. Firstly we need to try our hardest at everything we do – even if we think we are no good at it. The harder we try, the better we'll get, even if we're not the best in the class.

Secondly, if we are good at something, can we use that skill to help others, not just for ourselves?

Christians believe that every single person is important – not just the rich or famous or pretty or clever ones – every one of us has skills they can use in the world. This is one of the reasons Jesus came to live on the earth – to show everyone that they are special and important whatever they are good at.

Prayer

Dear God,
Thank you for the gifts and abilities you have given us. Help us to make the best use of them.
Amen.

Suggested songs

71 – God has a perfect plan for me
79 – God is the one who wants the best for me

News headlines

Aim

To think about the fact that we'll never understand everything about God.

Requirements

A few newspaper headlines either on large sheets of card or acetate sheets but with one significant word missing (have a few serious ones as well as some funny ones).

Volunteers

Ask for some volunteers to hold up the headlines.

Ask the children to guess the missing words.

There seems to be more bad news than good in the papers these days. Christians believe that God is a God of love, but how can this be so when babies die, innocent people suffer and terrible things happen? When we read about these things it is very easy to doubt whether God exists at all – let alone him being a God of love. In these situations perhaps we shouldn't even try to find answers.

Application

There is a verse in the Bible which says, 'Trust in the Lord with all your heart and don't depend on your own understanding.' (Proverbs 3:5)

It is not wrong to have doubts and question things we believe, especially when it comes to God. There are some things that even people who have been Christians for a very long time don't understand.

We need to remember that when things happen which make us doubt God, the Bible tells us that God is hurting with us and wants to help us. We just have to be honest with him and ask him to help – just like asking a friend or someone you trust.

Prayer

Dear God,
Please help us to trust you with things in our lives which we don't

understand. Thank you that you care about us and everything that happens to us.
Amen.

Suggested songs   37 – Do not worry
46 – Everybody has a wobble

Oh, I just can't decide!

Aim To help us think about the choices we make.

Requirements The Friends Quiz (see page 38).

Volunteers 2 best friends

All of us, every day, have choices to make – can you name some; for example, what to wear, do, watch or eat?

I want to see how well you know your friends this morning and the sorts of choices they make.

The problem is that we may have to live with the consequences of the choices we make; if we eat too much chocolate we get fat, but sometimes the consequences may be more serious that that.

Application Christians believe that right at the beginning of time God created man and woman with the freedom to choose – between following him or doing things their way. With that freedom came a responsibility of having to live with the consequences of the things they chose. And from the moment they chose to do things their way things started to go wrong – murder, wars, famine, families falling out – the Bible is full of those sorts of stories. It was a bit like life today.

But Christians also believe that God had a choice. To either let people carry on getting into a bigger and bigger mess or to do something about it. And that's why Christians celebrate Easter – because God chose to act – sending Jesus to die on a cross and to come alive again. But Jesus had a choice too – he could have refused to die, he could have had fame and fortune, using the gifts God had given him. But the Bible says that Jesus chose to die, so that people everywhere could have a friendship with him if they wanted to.

What helps us to make the right choices, how do we decide what to do, or what not to do?

Remember, when you make a choice today, think carefully; it might not only be you that is affected by the choice you make.

Prayer

Dear God,
Please help us to make the right choices today and not just to copy whatever everyone else does.
Amen.

Suggested songs

17 – Be bold, be strong
36 – Dear Lord, my Father

THE FRIENDS QUIZ

What would your friend do?

1. Your friend's mum has agreed to take them out for a meal. Would they rather go to:

   A: McDonald's

   B: Burger King

   C: the local chippy

   D: an expensive restaurant?

2. Your friend has chosen McDonald's. Would they order:

   A: a Big Mac

   B: fries

   C: chicken nuggets

   D: hamburger?

3. After the meal your friend's mum offers to take them to buy their birthday present. Would they choose:

   A: a CD

   B: clothes

   C: a cuddly toy

   D: a video?

4. They choose a video. Would it be:

   A: something sloppy and romantic

   B: cartoons

   C: sport

   D: action?

(Swap over the person answering questions at this point)

5. Your friend's family has just won some money on the Lottery. Their mum offers to buy them a present. They choose:

   A: a TV

   B: a personal CD player

   C: clothes

   D: a new bike?

6. Your friend chooses clothes. Would they rather have:

   A: a new coat

   B: shoes

   C: an outfit for a special occasion

   D: new school clothes?

7. Still celebrating, each member of your friend's family is allowed to go somewhere for a treat. Does your friend choose:

A: a football match
B: the cinema
C: the theatre
D: a day out in London?

8. You and your friend are having an evening in and are watching a video. You offer to get something to eat. Does your friend choose:

A: crisps
B: popcorn
C: chocolate
D: nothing?

Prayer

Aim

To think about the fact that prayer is just talking to God.

Requirements

List of about 20 animals for a game of charades.
Prizes for winning team.

Volunteers

4 (2 teams)

Play a game of charades. (Send one team out of the room while the first performs to prevent cheating.)

See how many they can get right. (You could have TV programmes, animals, job, etc., as themes to act out.)

Application

We use all sorts of ways to communicate with each other – can anyone give me any ideas?

People have many different ways of communicating with God too. Some stand, some sit, others kneel. Some people use loud words, or old words like thee or thou. Some shout, some whisper, some people use no words at all. Everyone talks to God in different ways. The great thing is, if we follow Jesus' example in the Bible, prayer is talking to God just like I'm talking to you now. Jesus talked to his father about everything, just as if he were talking to a friend he could see. He used no special words and we can talk to God in the same way, about anything and everything. He is always listening.

Prayer

Dear God,
Thank you that we can talk to you about anything and everything.
Thank you for listening to us and answering our prayers.
Amen.

Suggested songs   286 – Prayer is like a telephone
381 – When you pray

Quiz time – Bible or not?

Aim

To think about the difference between pride and humility.

Requirements

List of sayings – some from the Bible – some not. (Use the ones following – or you may have something better!)

1. A nagging woman is like a dripping tap. (*Yes* – Proverbs 27:15)

2. As a dog goes back to his own vomit so a fool repeats his foolishness. (*Yes* – Proverbs 26:11)

3. Don't worry – be happy. (*No* – but in Matthew God says not to worry about tomorrow, trust in him.)

4. Money causes all kinds of evil. (*No* – in 1 Timothy 6:10 he says that the *love* of money is the root of evil.)

5. Whoever makes himself great will be humbled, whoever makes himself humble will be made great. (*Yes* – Matthew 23:12)

6. Pride goes before a fall. (*Yes* – pride goes before destruction and a proud spirit before a fall. Proverbs 16:18)

Volunteers

4

I thought it would be fun to have a quiz this morning. Which of the above six sayings appear in the Bible (*Yes*) and which do not (*No*)?

Application

Sometimes when I look in the Bible I'm surprised at just how many sayings there are: some that I wouldn't expect to find in the Bible; some that people have based sayings on and that are now used in everyday life; and some that have been passed down through the years from the times when people used to go to church and read the Bible much more than they do now.

I don't know if you were surprised or not that some of those sayings were in the Bible – have a look for yourselves sometime and see how many you can find.

I want us to think about the last two – about pride and humility. I looked both words up in a thesaurus and these are other words it came up with.

Pride: arrogant, boastful, self-important.
Humble: good-mannered, polite, selfless.

Of course, sometimes it's good to feel proud if we've done something well or achieved something that we've been working towards for a long time – that's great. We just need to be careful that that pride doesn't make us feel and act better than everyone else and cause us to start looking down on them.

Everyone here is different, all with different gifts and abilities, yet each person is as important as the next and deserves to be treated and respected the same as everyone else.

Let's try and be selfless rather than selfish, you'll be surprised at the difference it makes. As the Proverb says – those who are humble will be made great – think of someone in history or even today who you know who may be like that.

Prayer

Dear God,
Please help us to be humble and put other people before ourselves today.
Amen.

Suggested songs

65 – Give me a heart of compassion
364 – We wanna sing about your love

Really important?

Aim	To think about what is really important in our lives.
Requirements	A list of questions with 4 options of answers Sweets
Volunteers	1

Use the format of the TV programme *Who wants to be a millionaire?* using suitable questions for your audience and sweets as prizes – don't make the questions too hard. (If you can get hold of the theme music, even better.)

Application

If we are not careful we could go through life only concentrating on the things we haven't got, wanting more and more, so that everything else in our lives gets pushed to one side.

It's not wrong to want nice things but if we spend all our time wanting more then two things could happen: firstly we forget about the things we have and stop appreciating them, even though we might have so much more than other people; and secondly we might start ignoring people, or even worse, using the people who matter to us just for what we can get out of them, or what they can do for us.

Jesus took things a step further when he talked about our priorities in life. He said, 'The thing you should want is God's kingdom and doing what God wants and then everything else you need [food and clothes] will be given to you.' (Matthew 6:33)

Christians believe that if we find out about God and what he wants for us in our lives we won't be as bothered about material things.

How about spending some time this week thinking not about the things we want but about all the great things we already have and really appreciating them.

Prayer

Dear God,
Thank you for the great things you give us. Help us to appreciate them and not just want more and more.
Amen.

Suggested songs

56 – Father, I thank you
136 – I just want to thank you, Lord

Second chance (confessions)

Aim   To think about forgiveness

Requirements   3 or 4 'Confessions'

Either get hold of a copy of one of Simon Mayo's confession books (or perhaps you could ask a teacher – or even the Head! to relate their confessions!) and have a vote amongst the children to see if they think the person should be forgiven or not.

Application   It's quite easy to forgive someone when we aren't involved in the situation, when we are not being hurt. It's a lot harder when we are personally involved. All sorts of things go around in our head – why should we ever talk to that person again, let alone forgive them?

Listen to what the Bible says about how many times we should forgive someone:

Peter came to Jesus and asked, 'Lord when my fellow believer sins against me how often should I forgive him? Should I forgive him as much as seven times?' Jesus answered, 'I tell you, you must forgive him more than seven times. You must forgive him even if he does wrong to you 77 times.' (Matthew 18:21-22)

That's pretty heavy stuff! You see, Jesus knew that if we don't forgive people when they hurt us, it is we who suffer in the end. All those angry feelings we have against the person can end up festering inside us and ruin our lives, making us angry and bitter and even ill.

There are also more serious consequences of not forgiving someone. Listen again to what it says in the Bible:

If you forgive others of their wrong, your father in heaven will also forgive you for your wrong. But if you don't forgive others, your Father in heaven will not forgive you. (Matthew 6:14-15)

Prayer	Dear God, Help us to be the sort of people who are prepared to forgive others. Amen.
Suggested songs	9 – Amazing grace 83 – God never gives up

Temptations

Aim   To think about why Jesus had to die.

Requirements   3 doughnuts

Volunteers   3

I want us to think a little bit about why we celebrate Easter – why was it necessary for Jesus to die?

One of the biggest temptations when eating a doughnut is to lick your lips – so we are going to have a competition this morning to see how much of a doughnut each person can eat without falling into temptation – and licking their lips.

Give each person a doughnut – the one who finishes the whole doughnut without licking their lips is the winner.

Application   The Bible is full of stories of people who were offered the choice between right and wrong – to stand up for God, or to do their own thing. Sometimes they resisted temptation, at other times they gave in, often with serious consequences.

One of the most famous temptation stories in the Bible is that of Adam and Eve. They had it all – a beautiful place to live, no hard work to do and a very close friendship with God, and yet when they were tempted to disobey God they threw all this away by giving in too easily to temptation.

Christians believe very much in good and evil and the Bible is full of stories where the two met and all kinds of battles took place. Even Jesus was given the chance to give in to temptation – to either rule the world with his supernatural powers, or to die and complete God's plan. I wonder which we would have chosen?

The key to Easter lies in the choice Jesus made: he knew that the only way to win the fight between good and evil was for him to die. Jesus understands what it is like to be tempted, and to say no. He can help us when we have those difficult decisions to make – help us make the right choice.

Prayer

Dear God,
Thank you that you understand what it is like to be tempted. Please help us to be strong enough to say 'no' when we are faced with temptation.
Amen.

Suggested songs

62 – From heaven you came
198 – Jesus isn't dead any more

Unbelievable!

Aim   To think about the reason Jesus was here on earth.

Requirements A game that involves a target of some sort
A blindfold

Volunteers   1

Blindfold the volunteer and see how many they can score on your target game when they cannot see.

Application   It's very difficult to hit something when you can't see it. It can also be difficult to go through life if you don't have something to aim at – a goal or a vision.

The people in history who have really made a difference have been those with a vision, knowing what they wanted to achieve and going for it – people like William Wilberforce, who fought to put an end to the slave trade, and other people whom you may have learnt about in history lessons who tried hard to make a difference.

Jesus was a man with a vision when he was here on earth, in fact he often talked about it. Listen to what he said: 'I must go to Jerusalem and suffer much . . . I will be put to death but three days later I will be raised to life.'

What a strange vision to have, suffering and dying. The thing was, Jesus' vision went further than dying because he knew he was going to come alive again. Lots of people today think it was impossible for Jesus to come back to life and that the Easter story is just that, a story someone made up.

Yet the Bible says that hundreds of people saw Jesus die, thousands saw him when he came alive again and millions of people all over the world have heard the story of Jesus and it has changed their lives.

Are we prepared to dismiss Easter as just another story or are we prepared to look into the evidence ourselves? Check it out, you might be surprised at what you find.

Prayer

Dear God,
Help us to find out the truth of the Easter story for ourselves and see the difference Jesus has made to the world.
Amen.

Suggested songs

45 – Easter jubilation
297 – Sing a song, sing a joyful song

Valentine's Day

Aim Thinking about the things we say, and how people are affected by them.

Requirements Cards with chat-up lines on.
Marshmallows (cut in half is probably best!)

Volunteers 4, plus 2 more to hold up pieces of card.

Girls sit facing the boys and they take it in turn to read out the chat-up lines. Before they say each line they have to place a marshmallow in their mouth. (It may be a good idea to have an empty bin handy!)

The rest of the school vote on the best pair at chatting each other up.

Boys	*Girls*
You are lovely	You are so sensitive
Your hair is like golden straw	Your muscles are so rippling
When you look at me I go weak at the knees	Your voice is so deep and sexy
I love the way you smile	You are so rugged and handsome
I love you, darling	I will love you for ever

Application That was just a bit of fun, but I want us to think about the things we say to each other. Often it is a lot easier to say something destructive and unpleasant and hurtful than something encouraging and kind.

All of us have been hurt at some time by something someone has said about us or to us, yet we continue to do the same to others. Listen to the advice in the Bible about what we should say to others:

When you talk do not say harmful things but say what people need – words that will help others be stronger, then what you say will do good to those who listen to you. (Ephesians 4:29)

I want to leave you with two challenges this morning:

How many people can you encourage or say something kind to today?

Stop and think how it feels before you say something unpleasant and hurtful to someone – it might just make the difference to their day.

Prayer

Dear God,
Please help us to think before we speak today and help us to find kind and encouraging things to say.
Amen.

Suggested songs

245 – Love, love your enemies
312 – Teach me to dance

What did you say?

Aim

To think about our anger.

Requirements

4 large balloons
4 pumps

Volunteers

3 or 4 (tell them they need to be very brave)

Give each volunteer a large balloon. See who can blow up the balloon with a pump until it bursts.

Application

Have you ever felt like that balloon? Sometimes we get so annoyed, so angry, that we just can't hold it back any longer until . . . BANG! we explode and all the anger comes pouring out. Sometimes we can rightly get angry, for example at injustice, or when people are starving or homeless, and this anger should spur us on to do something about it. Usually though, we get angry and we say things we regret, we do things we wish we hadn't and generally lose control. We hurt other people and we hurt ourselves. Our anger doesn't just damage other people, it can spoil our lives as well.

Sometimes people bottle up their anger inside. They might have been angry about something or another person for years and although they might have forgotten what they were angry about to start with, the feeling is just eating away inside them and ruining their lives.

Christians believe that God helped other people to write the Bible so that it could guide us in the way we live our lives; it's full of helpful advice for people like you and me. Listen to what it says about anger and losing our tempers.

If you stay calm you are wise, but if you have a hot temper, you only show how stupid you are. (Proverbs 29:11)

Do not use harmful words, only helpful ones, the kind that build up and encourage, so that what you say will do good to those who hear you. (Ephesians 4:29)

Christians believe that if we want him to, God can help us put this advice into practice in our lives.

Prayer

Dear God,
Please help us to control our anger today and to walk away if we get wound up.
Amen.

Suggested songs

248 – Make me a channel of your peace
304 – Some things make you angry

X-ray vision – what is the consequence?

Aim	To think about the consequences of our actions.
Requirements	6 pieces of paper 6 pens
Volunteers	6

Give six volunteers a piece of paper and a pen each. Get them to write at the top of the paper their answer to question 1, fold the paper over just enough to cover the writing and then pass it on to the person sitting next to them who writes the answer to question 2, and then repeat the process for each question. After the last question pass the paper on once more and get the volunteers to read out their consequence with you adding the words in italics. (You may need to warn the children to be careful about the things they write down.)

1. Name a famous person (man)
   Met
2. Name a second famous person (woman)
   At
3. Where did they meet?
   He gave her
4. What did the man give the woman? (object)
   She gave him
5. What did the woman give back? (object)
   The consequences were
6. What happened as a result? (consequence of their actions)

Application

How often do we do or say something without thinking of the consequences of our actions first? Sometimes, perhaps, we may just upset one person and the consequences of our actions may be quite small. Other times we may affect things on a much larger scale. Take the world we live in. How often do we abuse it by not recycling things or by throwing our rubbish around or by being careless when we are in the countryside?

Take our friends and family: how often do we hurt them by the things we do or say, because we do something without thinking of the consequences.

Let's remember to think before we act, and realise that our actions may have all sorts of consequences, good and bad.

Prayer
Dear God,
Help us to realise that our actions and words have consequences, and to think before we speak or act.
Amen.

Suggested songs
17 – Be bold, be strong
312 – Teach me to dance

Yes or no?

Aim
To think about the Christian God being the only one.

Requirements
A stopwatch or watch with a second hand

Volunteers
3-4

How long can you have a conversation with the volunteers without them using the words yes or no?

I want to take a look today at some of the things God said about himself.

It was really hard not to use the words yes or no in the game, but in life things are even more difficult. There is often a middle ground.

Application
Christians believe that when it comes to God there is no middle ground; we have to decide for ourselves whether he exists or not, either he does or he doesn't – there is no space in between.

The Old Testament part of the Bible is full of stories of men and women who were sure God did exist and should be followed, and some of them even risked their lives because they believed in him.

God said he was the only god. In Isaiah 45:5 he tells a king, 'I am the Lord and there is no other, apart from me there is no God.'

We need to decide for ourselves, does God exist, yes or no?

Prayer
Dear God,
Help us to take time to discover for ourselves whether you are real or not.
Amen.

Suggested songs   96 – Have we made our God too small?
196 – Jesus is greater than the greatest heroes

Zoo time (modelling balloons)

Aim To think about how God can change us.

Requirements 8 modelling balloons
2 pumps

Volunteers 4

Give each person two inflated modelling balloons (most good party shops sell them – you may need a pump!) Give them two minutes to create something from their balloons. Choose a winner in the way you think most appropriate for your audience!

Application Balloons are great for changing into things – as we have just seen. But do you ever wish you could change yourself? Maybe it's something about your appearance you don't like, or you wish you were good at something that you find difficult; it could be a number of different things – perhaps things that only you know about.

God made it clear in the Bible that he isn't interested in our outward appearance, it's what goes on in our heart that concerns him. When God's people were looking for a king God showed them someone who would be just right for the job – David. On the outside he may have looked small and skinny and not up to much, but on the inside God knew he was the right man for the job.

Christians believe that Jesus died on the cross not just so that we could be forgiven for all the wrong things we do in our lives but also so that we might be able to ask Jesus to help us to change – not necessarily on the outside, but on the inside, our attitudes and behaviour, the things that really count.

Prayer

Dear God,
Please help us to be the sort of people who are prepared to be changed on the inside, where it really matters.
Amen.

Suggested songs

97 – Have you got an appetite?
130 – If we admit to God